A Prayer Companion Through Cancer

Kate Strickland

Onwards and Upwards Publishers

3 Radfords Turf
Cranbrook
Exeter
EX5 7DX
United Kingdom

www.onwardsandupwards.org

This first edition published in the United Kingdom by Onwards and Upwards Publishers (2018).

ISBN: 978-1-78815-671-4
Editor: Honor Parkinson
Cover design: LM Graphic Design

Printed in the United Kingdom.

About the Author

Kate Strickland comes from Cheshire, England. After graduating from UEA with a degree in English Literature, she spent over ten years in management roles in the North West of England, including an Architects' practice and a FTSE 100 company.

Now married, with two children, Kate commits her time to her writing, her Charity Trustee work, her role of Chair of Governors to a large school and, most importantly, her family.

Endorsements

Prayers become real when they are carved from experience. In this book Kate has brought a lived experience to God, and the result is a collection of prayers that should help people at all stages of the journey with cancer. Honest, hopeful and – yes – joyful in the face of darkness and pain, it points us to the cross, and to the life eternal that the cross has won for us all. I am most grateful to Kate for quarrying, shaping and polishing these prayers so that we can all use them.

Paul Bayes
Bishop of Liverpool

Sharing a cancer journey with someone you love and adore is heartbreaking, exhausting and, at times, overwhelming. I travelled this journey with my brave and beautiful daughter Tasha. At every turn, with every step, Kate's prayers supported us. Her words gave us strength and hope and reminded us that our Lord was always with us. Kate sent us a prayer before we faced every challenge; when we received the initial devastating diagnosis, when we were in the darkest of places, but also when we received encouraging news and when we felt so grateful for those who were caring for us. I know that the prayers Kate has collected in this beautiful book will help so many others on their personal cancer journey.

Christine Marsland

Being diagnosed with cancer is a very personal and unique experience. No two people will have the same experience, no two people will react in the same way, no two families will deal with it in the same way. One thing, however, is constant and sure and that is the love of God. Being upheld by others in prayer, knowing we can come to God in our darkest hours with our deepest fears, longings and hopes can be transformative. The prayers in this book are hard won. Dip into this pool and take the water of healing and refreshment you need. I commend them to you.

Rev. Dr Sarah Baker
Stage 3 oesophageal cancer survivor

Contents

For darling Natasha –

encourager, prayer companion and warrior

Naked

God of Truth, I come to you laid bare in my fear, for only in your eyes am I stripped naked of my disguise of normality.

Lord, you know my deep desire and longing for good results and you sense my growing fear now consuming me inside.

Lord, you also know the steps ahead.

You are already in the laboratory testing room, you already know the results, you are already guiding my physician and you are already in my life path ahead, whatever that may be.

I come to you as your child and ask you to accompany me on my journey ahead.

Be close to me as I receive my test results, whether a relief or devastating, and make my life's journey a pilgrimage with you.

Please stay by my side as I await my diagnosis.

Help me to breathe, eat, speak and rest, and hold me in your steadfast embrace when I learn of my results.

I place myself and all of my burdens into your loving hands and commit myself to you.

In the name of your son, our saviour Jesus Christ.

Amen.

I Have Some Bad News...

Eternal God,

I have fallen down to the depths after learning of my diagnosis with cancer.

I am remote, outside of myself, low and fearful.

I am overcome with panic.

I cannot think clearly, I cannot rest, my tears fall and it feels that there is no escape.

As I plummet to the expanse and extremes of my despair, may I focus on this single prayer: that my faith in you will protect and sustain me, even when I shout out in anger and disbelief to you.

May I land on you as my rock, my rock of salvation, steadfast and unmoving.

I need you to be at the base of this seemingly bottomless pit, as I am in freefall.

Be a solid foundation upon which to lift my head, learn to crawl and eventually take the necessary steps ahead.

I desperately need you to be unshakable, perpetual in your love and grounding, as my world feels as though it is blown apart, without warning, sense or reason.

I am numb. I am longing for escape from this monster within. This horrible, beastly cancer is terrifying me and here without invitation.

I am violated.

Be with my family and friends as they too absorb their shock, their anger and their numbness. I need them all so very much in the days, weeks and months ahead. Please uphold them in their anguish, so that they too can uphold me.

Remain constant, my steadfast rock, my Holy Father.

In the name of Jesus.

Amen.

Acceptance

I accept my diagnosis, Lord, and I will carry my cross.

Its weight seems insurmountable but I ask that you, please, help me with my burden.

I accept that this is my journey and I ask that you accompany me on my path.

My resistance and anger are placing a strain on my poor body and I must preserve my energy and regain my strength from you when I am crushed in spirit, for the journey ahead.

I know my path is a difficult one and I long for you, Lord, to carry me when the days feel untenable and for you to be the light in my darkness.

When I thirst for comfort, quench my needs, Lord, with your overwhelming peace and grace.

May I drink in your splendour and majesty and may my needs be met by you.

In your holy name.

Amen.

Fear

Heavenly Father,

When I am afraid, walk alongside me.

When I am in pain, hold me in your arms.

When I feel alone, remind me that I am part of your family.

When I am angry, hear my dismay.

When I feel like I can't take another step, carry me, Lord.

Loving and comforting God, in whose eternal arms I rest, I bring to you myself, my family and friends.

You alone are God Almighty and the source of our longing.

You alone hear the lament and anguish of my heart.

May your light surround me.

May your love enfold me.

May your power protect me.

May your presence watch over me.

For wherever I am, you are too.

In the name of Christ.

Amen.

Companionship

Father, Protector, Sovereign Lord,

How I have prayed for positive news; oh Lord, the longing in my heart is overwhelming. How painful my fear and waiting were – and now my diagnosis feels like a defeat.

It drains me – it consumes me, Lord – and I am sinking, plummeting down into an abyss of fear.

Take me, Lord, your blessed child, on this next day in my journey, the path of which is unknown to me, but is all in your sight.

Only you, Lord, know the secrets of our hearts; only you, Lord, know our destiny, as you are already there before us, until our eternity. Just as you knit each of us together in the womb, so too you know our entire body's life before we are born.

May I remember that whatever happens you will sustain me in my journey, surrounded by the care of my loved ones.

Be my advocate, my countenance, my Father.

Be my constant companion.

Life can seem to be insurmountable on these days.

Lord, please carry me.

Amen.

Why?

Why me, God?

Why choose me?

My heart breaks with my love for you, my love for my life and that you could allow this to happen.

Why have you forsaken me?

Remind me of your promise of Paradise, and fill me with the Holy Spirit to wash my anger away.

I will gaze upon you, Lord, on earth in my prayers, and will one day see your beautiful face in heaven.

Why *not* me, Lord?

Wash me clean of my need to blame, and wipe my tears with your presence and overwhelming love.

Be with me in my lament and guide me through my all-consuming persecution.

Why would you commit your mighty love to me?

Why me, God?

I am blessed.

Amen.

Silently Screaming

I'm screaming inside and nobody can hear my screams.

I can't even let the noise out, but inside it gets louder and louder.

Deafening, silent rage.

What have I done to deserve this?

What have I done wrong?

The cancer is near, a monster inside.

All I feel now is a screaming, yelling monster of rage inside me.

Don't let me become the cancer's beast, Lord, perpetuating its sadness, anger and nastiness.

May my tears wash me clean of this hurt and anger, and may your love flow within me, cleansing my resentment away.

This is a trial, this is my Gethsemane, and I turn to you in prayer, on my knees for your direction.

May my tears wash away my anger and fill my body with the Holy Spirit.

Grant me the gift of your grace to overcome this inner hostility.

In Jesus' name.

Amen.

Tests

Father God,

Thank you for every moment of my life, be it good or bad, as I know I am only here in your name.

I also know that whatever time I am going through, when all is stripped away – possessions, friendships, health and security – that you are my endless peace.

As I lay my life before you, please fill me with your light, calm and fortitude.

As I go today to the clinic, please be with me.

May Jesus be my constant companion, and your grace be my very breath.

I pray, Lord, for good test results and healing for my body and I thank you for being my constant companion on this hard, hard journey, even in times of my anger or despair.

Fill me with your light, your unending light; and renew my faith, my spirit, and strengthen my soul.

In the name of Jesus.

Amen.

Results

Father, Protector, Sovereign Lord,

Life can seem so unsurmountable on days like today, but I know, Lord, that you are always with me; I can never be alone.

Thank you for my friends and family, and for their love and solidarity.

Thank you for the gift of my life so far.

Make me see the blessing of each day, no matter how hard it seems.

I know only you understand my anguish, just as you did your own son, our saviour, as he suffered that we may live. He died on the cross that we may have hope; divine and heavenly hope through Jesus, who is with me now and will be with me forever and me with him.

God bless me, strengthen me, fortify me and guide me.

Comfort my family and friends; draw them into your loving arms.

In the name of your son, my saviour Jesus Christ. Amen.

Looking Ahead

Father God,

I know your unending commitment to me as your child and I humbly give you thanks every day of my life.

I know, Father, that you are already in the consulting room of the hospital with my doctor – you are guiding their thoughts – already in the treatment room with the nurses, enabling their work, and already watching over me with your abiding love, which never fails.

I pray for positive results today and I pray for the steps forward to be clearer to me so I can accept their necessity, however brutal they may or may not be.

I know you're already in those steps ahead too.

Hold me, strengthen me, fortify me, and may I sense your presence and peaceful balm this day.

May my family and friends know your peace. I am so grateful for them and for my relationship with you; my thanks can never seem sufficient.

Through you, my Father, and in humility.

Amen.

Longing

Heavenly Father,

I long for good news; my heart just aches for something to relieve this panic and pressure inside. It's building and building and I just want to scream.

My longing is so strong, it leaves me speechless.

May my tears be my unsaid prayers to you as I struggle to find my words or even catch my breath.

Whatever happens today, be with me, my Lord, my Father, my Protector, in the name of your son, Jesus Christ.

May I know your unending and unfathomable grace and peace this day and always.

Amen.

Before Surgery

Creator Father,

As I await my surgery, my mind is polluted by anxiety and trepidation.

I am fearful, Lord, and seek your blessed assurance and peace.

Help me find the courage to face my surgery.

Having listened to my consultant, I am sure that this is the right process for me and to enable my life to move forwards.

Be with the surgeon, Lord, with their God-given gifts and learned wisdom, to provide me with the best surgical outcome.

Be with the nurses as they provide my care and comfort in the days and weeks ahead.

Thank you for all the gifts of physicians, hospitals and nurses, a privilege denied to many.

I know that my friends and family are anxious and fearful too. They will be awake and waiting for news as I sleep and slip into a place of unawareness. This journey is a brutal one for them too, and they also need an intimacy with you to find peace, fortitude and the strength which can only emanate from you.

I pray for a successful surgery and for healing in your holy name.

Amen.

After Surgery

Panic has turned to pain,

Anxiety has turned to aching,

And once more I look to you.

Once more my heart turns to you.

Thank you for bringing me safely through my surgery, and now, as I begin my process of recovery, I want to be still in your presence; I want to be silent in wonder of you and I want to praise you, Father, through this pain.

I am yet to know, Father, what the outcome of my surgery is, but I know that whatever that is, you will stand with me through this trial.

I thank you, Lord.

Absorb me in my quiet time with you and help me to cast aside the noise of hospital, machines and busyness; help me through this discomfort and disquiet, with my eyes fixed on you and your unending peace.

In the name of Jesus Christ.

Amen.

From the Depths

Eternal Father,

I pray now and earnestly ask that I may feel your deep grace and peace once again.

On my knees, I put my faith in you to deliver me out of the deep, stormy and murky depths of darkness, as your love for me as your child is so huge, wide and deep, calm and clear.

I ask that you pull me to calmer waters where I feel able to tread water again and draw breath.

I am drowning in sorrow and need you as my buoy, my balance and my sustainer.

Just as you parted the seas, now occupy this ocean; command it and deliver me to safety.

Thank you for your grace.

Thank you for hearing my prayer.

Thank you for watching over me now as I rest.

Fill my body with your Holy Spirit so that I may feel your presence right now.

Make my body warm again in the knowledge of your constant companionship in my life, even at times of anguish, anger, sadness or pain.

Your love is unconditional for your children.

I ask this is the name of your son, Jesus Christ, whose suffering meant that I can live in the certain knowledge of my eternal home.

Amen.

For New Treatments

Holy and ever faithful Father,

Be with me as I go to the clinic today for treatment once again.

As I see in autumn the leaves fade, fall and their goodness seep into the ground to sit quietly until the new spring, I am reminded that yours is a world of constant renewal.

Change is all part of your master plan for the beauty that surrounds us; the vivid autumnal yellows, browns and reds, and the white and the cold sky as winter approaches.

We too are made in your goodness and as parts of our lives change, new processes start and new beginnings emerge.

May my old cells accept this treatment and wait for their renewal over the difficult coming days.

Lord, what a hard and long process this is, but I wait with a resolute inner confidence in my faith that you will remain steadfast with me.

Be with me in my constant prayers for renewal, for the springtime of my health once more and my healing.

On my knees I humbly worship you, I delight in your goodness and I ask for rebirth, healing and a new spring all over your world, to see your glory and your kingdom.

Be with the bereaved this day.

Be with the war-torn.

Be with the lonely and suffering.

Show your radiant glory once again in those parts of the world in which your son walked.

Suffering in this world is not just here in my life; may my prayers be for all in pain and anguish this day.

In the name of Jesus.

Amen.

For My Family

How blessed I am to be part of my family;

How blessed I am to have the support from them that I do.

I give thanks every day for their presence, their love and their support.

I give thanks to you, Lord, as my eternal Father, head of all our households.

As we are in this time of change, brought on by my illness, may we be reminded that you are a God of change and transformation, Father, Son and Holy Spirit.

The seasons change; winter fades with the hope of spring. The leaves wither and fall leaving the trees naked in their vulnerability. My family and I are made vulnerable and laid bare by this cancer.

Be with me, Lord, when I feel guilt and despair at what I cannot do for my family, that this illness in me has caused such change, especially when my treatments, surgery or medications affect my ability to be present for my family.

At this time, remind them through their memories and love for me of my unending love for them and my overwhelming desire to get well again for them all.

I know that this journey is not mine alone and that all our lives have changed for ever. May we in time accept this change, rather than rally against it.

Please be the vine that binds us together through the most trying and difficult days and nights.

I pray for my family's safety, their peace, their fellowship and that they may feel the blessing and security of your love as I do,

A love which brings me tremendous comfort,

Just as Mary did for her son, a love that weeps with me in my Gethsemane.

We are all part of your family, Lord, and may my earthly, womb-knitted kin know you are their shelter and solace too.

In the name of Jesus.

Amen.

For My Partner

Lord, we live our lives together, looking forward to our future and smiling together at our past, and then this – this wretched cancer, a parasite on both our hearts.

May our unity, love and desire for each other prove insurmountable to this disease. Love must conquer all and love is sometimes all we have.

How we need each other more than ever, and yet how separate this disease can at times make us feel.

Let us embrace through the pain, weep in unity, and when we feel anger may we remember we are on this life path together and to not channel that frustration and dismay at each other.

On days when all I can do is breathe, let our love be a hand-hold, or a kiss or a prayer.

We know, Lord, that with you love is all, love conquers all, and our love will remain through it all.

Please uphold our love, commitment and relationship through the toughest of days.

Overwhelm any sense of inadequacies, jealousies or anger; instil love, peace and togetherness.

Some days I feel such guilt that my body and the disease within it affects us both so much; this is not just a physical disease, I carry it emotionally.

Please remind me, and calm my heart by your presence, that I have not chosen this journey, I am not culpable, I am not the disruptor.

We are on a bend in the road and the path ahead is not clear; we need to walk forward together.

Unity, love, commitment.

Love: there is no greater gift from you.

In your loving name, I pray; and into your arms I fall in my humility.

Amen.

For My Physician

How mighty you are, Lord, to create and give wisdom to your children –

Wisdom enough to alter lives, determine outcomes and aid the sick.

May my physician be clear in their dialogue with me, that I may understand my treatment options.

Grant them the courage to be candid, whilst kind, in guiding me in my outcomes, and enable them to seek new possibilities to give hope to me and other patients.

When they leave the hospital each day, guide them safely home and be with them in their rest and leisure.

May your blessings be with them and their families, and may your comfort abound in them on days when they deliver difficult news to patients, or absorb and relate bad or disappointing results.

They too are flesh alone and your mighty sustenance and guidance allows them to promote healing, recovery or remission and palliative care.

Thank you, God, for the gifts of wisdom, compassion and courage for my physician and many other medical professionals.

In Lord Jesus' name.

Amen.

For My Nurses

Long days, late nights, they look after us so well.

Every day they leave their homes and their families and come to a place to care;

People they haven't met yet,

People they have cared for a longer time now.

They treat patients with patience and dignity; they care and they use their gifts to help others beyond any job description on paper.

A smile, an encouragement and a supportive ear.

They hear each story, they see sadness and desperation in eyes and faces, and their commitment and care raises smiles, brings comfort and helps people take difficult steps.

Their acts of care, support, compassion and their knowledge and practice of treatments make them the warriors who aid our fight, our accomplices in battle when we cannot face the fight.

How hard their job is, how important their job is! Shield them and may your light be their armour.

I thank you, Lord, for the gift of all nurses and care professionals.

May they know that their determination to maintain dignities, to support and encourage during tears, and their ability to explain and administer new or old treatments, is so crucial, so necessary and so appreciated.

Angels on earth, may they know your grace, your presence, your comfort on days where they weep, days when they come to work with worries at home of their own, and keep them safe in their daily lives.

Father, hear my prayer. Amen.

For My Children

Lord,

If am I scared, then how do my children feel?

How can I help them to understand?

I am their parent, but as your child I seek your support and reassurance.

From their first breath, I have been in awe of their creation.

From their first heartbeat, I have been forever grateful for this blessing.

I want to actively be their parent, I want to comfort them and I want to care for them. At times that is hard or close to impossible because of my treatment or sickness.

I will try to be open and not envious of others who are helping with my role, for these angels are helping me, not replacing me, and I must see that.

The one gift in all this that I pray is learnt and known by my children is the gift of gratitude;

Gratitude and thankfulness for every single second, every single breath, every single heartbeat.

May this journey teach them how to praise you in every storm, by my example in prayer to you this day; may they know that I am sustained by my relationship with you.

When I cannot perform tasks help me to pray with them and teach them of your ways and help their discipleship with you.

May they be blessed with gratitude for all that they love, may they praise you for their health, may they respect the gift of their body and may they learn how to come alongside and draw near to those who are suffering and show their support and compassion as adults.

Lord, I pray that however my journey progresses they will always know my deep and unconditional love for them.

We will never be apart, as your children, just as I am part of them and they are part of me. Near or far, we are as one in your name.

Protect them, nurture them and sustain them as their Father.

In the name of Jesus Christ.

Amen.

Times of Waiting

If I wasn't so numb I would scream.

The waiting is unbearable.

The waiting.

The not knowing.

Each slow second contains a what if...

What if?

What should I have done?

If only I had...

I could just run away.

If I ran away would all this be left behind?

I long for the waiting to end and yet I don't want to know the answers.

I'm in a no man's land; anything is possible and anything could be.

You are in everything, Lord; you are in every second, even when they feel like a lifetime.

You are in every possibility.

You have been there from the start of time and you are forever.

Give me hope, Lord, to dream of the possibilities.

Give me courage, Lord, to face the realties ahead.

Give me the gift of patience, Lord, in this time of apprehension and anxiety.

May you always be my now; be my expectation, be my future, with your blessed assurances from cradle to grave of the constancy of your love and commitment to me.

In the name of your son, Jesus Christ, whose name and might is eternal.

Amen.

Bad Results

Father God,

I am so disappointed and disheartened.

I am crushed.

I had hoped and prayed for good results and now I receive this news.

What have I done wrong?

Why is this happening to me?

Please help me to understand that this cancer is not of you, it is not a punishment for some wrongdoing, it is not a sign that you do not care for me.

Please help me, Lord, as I accept and understand my results better as my shock falls aside.

May my tears fall as prayers to you; may my anger be overshadowed by my knowledge of your love, and the hope that it brings in this life and the next.

I thank you for your constancy and companionship at this dreadful time.

May my consultants be blessed as they help and guide me at this time, aided by the loyal and angelic nurses who administer my care and treatment.

It is so hard, Lord, when I am trying to be well, and I am desperately longing to be well for all who care for me. This journey is painful for them too and they share my sadness and crushed spirit.

Bind up our wounds of heart with your mighty hands.

In your holiest name I pray, Creator God.

Amen.

The Night Before Results

Almighty God and Deliverer,

Be with my family and me in our homes tonight and guide us into peaceful rest.

As we rest, surround us with your light, love and protection.

Surround our beds with your angels and the balm of the Holy Spirit.

Send your grace into our very beings tonight, that we may sense your presence with us as we rest, and your fortitude and courage when we wake, and the love and support of all those who care for us.

I pray for positive results tomorrow.

I pray for less sickness come morning and I pray my thanks to you, Lord, for our lives and this our family, with our love for each other.

In Christ Jesus' name.

Amen.

Thank You for Good Results

Father God,

I have been given good news, and all good things come from you.

I praise you, Father, at this time of reprieve and I am forever humbled by your mercies.

May I take this time to pray for all other cancer patients in the world.

On this day of my good results, some people will be receiving their initial devastating diagnoses, some will be receiving bad results and others will be losing their lives.

This disease, this cancer, is not of you, but our lives are.

You are with us at all these times to sustain us, support us, and when it is our time, carry us home to our eternity with you.

May my good results give me this opportunity, as an act of faith and thankfulness, to pray for all cancer patients worldwide, young and old.

I pray for improved access to treatments and continued developments in research and treatment.

You are mighty, Lord, and you give knowledge enough to your children to make these advances.

Thank you for this day and for my positive results.

I am hugely blessed and humbled without end,

Your servant in Christ, united in prayer with all those suffering.

Amen.

Hope in Suffering

The gift of hope is yours, Lord.

It is so hard to feel hopeful on the dark days of this journey, when I search, hungrily and in need for your light.

May my hope come in my perseverance through my treatments, sickness, weakness and fatigue.

I will persevere in your name.

Hold

On,

Pain

Ends.

Hope. Eternal, radical, God-given hope.

I will see your glory, Lord. I will be without pain and in that knowledge, I will hold on in my suffering,

Through the suffering of my saviour on the cross, and my prayers of thanks to you for the gift of him.

Amen.

Longing

With every hour of my life missed for treatment, every conversation missed for sickness, and every day affected by cancer, I long for normality.

I long to talk about other things than treatments and sickness, hospital visits and schedules.

Oh, to have a normal day, at home or at work, and to not be a cancer patient!

Oh, to be able to look the same again, to feel the same way again, to breathe in unhindered breaths and walk free of the shackles of this disease!

I long for normality, but I also long for you; to see your face and to feel the warmth of your embrace, Lord.

I pray for your acceptance of this frail body and mind, here on earth and, when my time comes, in your Paradise.

My heart aches with my longing.

Please comfort me, Lord.

Amen.

Drawing Near to God in Quiet

Be in my home.

Be in my room.

Sit by me on my bed and draw near to me, Lord.

My knowledge of your unending love is like a gentle breath on my face.

The warmth in my heart is my knowledge of drawing closer to you.

I am still, Lord; I am just me, alone in this bed and on this earth, but encircled by you.

May people of light and glory surround me as I rest, and their heavenly voices sing their praises and prayers to you.

May the stillness and silence be a foretaste of your mesmerising glory.

I can feel you here, Lord; I can feel the light of my heavenly guardians.

Be with me and stay with me evermore.

Amen.

Recovery

Each step is a torment.

Each wake up is a shock.

I am low with treatment and in your glorious name I pray for recovery for my body.

May every weakened cell be renewed by your love and light.

May my weight return to healthy levels, my organs recover from the toll of my treatment and, as I rest, my body gain energy enough to be able to function once again;

Small steps for me ahead, and for now it is enough to just breathe.

May those steps and inhalations grow in confidence and strength;

Small challenges will result in accomplishment.

You make all things new and in my recovery I lift my weak and frail body to you as an act of commitment and worship.

In Lord Jesus' name.

Amen.

Remission

Holy Father, I praise you.

You amaze me.

You have never left me.

You are my healer, and my words are insufficient in my awe of you.

Thank you for this gift of healing and all the opportunities it brings to me that I wondered if I would ever have again.

My blessings are huge and so may I now be a blessing to those I know who are in need.

I have received so much support and I pray for the wisdom and compassion to draw alongside others in their difficulties and needs.

Holy Father, I pray for all those suffering with cancer and visualise their healing.

I pray for their families and friends who suffer so much too.

I pray for their opportunities of treatment, that their days might contain the light of your glory and their sorrows contain the balm of your peace, presence and love.

In the name of our Father,

Amen.

Envy for Normality

It is the simple things that I miss the most:

Work, evenings out, being able to function in a normal way at home.

Oh Lord, how I long to prepare a meal, do a school pick-up, garden, shop, walk or swim.

I long for normality so much that the pain is physical.

I long for the freedom of choice of normal life without the confines of physical ability and treatment plans.

My weakness is too much to allow normality; this is my current, my now.

Please draw alongside me, Lord, in this pause from normality, and help me to embrace the snippets of the life I long for.

May every embrace feel lengthy; give me the strength to play with my children or chat on the phone, even if just for moments.

Help me, Lord, to resist my feeling of jealousy and envy of those whose lives go on unchanged. I know they have not forgotten me, even though sometimes those thoughts enter my mind.

In my small moments of reprieve or snippets of energy, fill my heart with so much joy that it overflows, for in this darkness I can see the light, joy and miracle of life so much more clearly, and I know this renewed vision and light can only come from you.

I know that you are near me, Lord, and I give you unending praise for your awesome might and majesty.

In Jesus' name.

Amen.

For Life with the Beast

I have been attacked further by this beast within.

I could cry out with hatred, but I turn in prayer to you to resist this overwhelming rage.

My body has become its cage and I pray for its release.

If I could tear it out with my own hands I would, this pernicious, nasty beast within.

With it, it brought darkness, its anger and its fury.

It came without invitation and I long for it to leave.

Overwhelm me with your Holy Spirit.

Drown its cries with your heavenly peace.

Quench its thirst with your glory and splendour.

Make me a vessel for your love, light and healing.

In Jesus' name.

Amen.

Prayers

I have lost control, but I will pray.

May my prayers have power and may they bring me closer to you.

This disease cannot remove my ability to pray; though it strips me of much else, may my prayers become stronger.

When I have no words, may my silence be full of your praise and honour.

The gift of prayer empowers me, relieves me and restores me.

When I am at a loss or desolate, my prayers refocus me and provide stability.

Thank you, Lord, for receiving my prayers and for the constant and everlasting friendship and companionship you give to me.

Through my prayers, I know that I am never alone.

My prayer today is of nothing but thanks to you.

Amen.

Why Me?

What did I do to deserve this?

Where did I go wrong?

I have tried to live a good life and then this.

Lord, I pray that you eradicate this introspection, this self-questioning, this self-doubt.

May I know that this cancer is not of you, it is not punishment for wrongdoing.

You gave me the gift of life, and the vessel that is my body.

Something has gone wrong and nobody knows why.

You are the creator of life, not death.

You are loving, not vengeful, and I am your child, regardless of my flaws and wrongdoings.

Please forgive me, Father, of all of my sins and place me in your glory.

My disease is not from you.

You sustain me and protect me.

Why would you do that?

Why me?

May my questioning be about the amazing gift of your love.

You love me so much... Why me?

What did I do to deserve this?

Thank you, Father. Amen.

Seeing the World Anew

Father God,

On a cold and wet morning when I find myself sat parked in traffic, watching the world rush around, I pray.

Places to go, meetings to attend and people to see.

Many people are going about their daily business without pause for thought or reflection or to revere your holy name.

None of these people know what the day ahead may bring; many assume they do.

Guide them, Lord, in their dreams to clarity of living.

Sometimes, Lord, when we are surrounded by difficulty and the blackness of uncertainty, it is so easy to be swallowed up whole by sadness, especially when the world around us continues to move at pace, without stopping to breathe or to sit a while with us in our place of distress and disease.

May I, as your blessed child, draw alongside all those who are suffering this day, all those who feel like their world has stopped, through my prayers and solidarity with you.

You sent your son, our saviour, who taught us how to pray; we know the road ahead can be difficult, and as we fall in despair we also fall on our knees, the perfect position to pray.

May I sit a while in prayer with all those suffering from cancer, drawing them to you and surrounding them with your light and glory; the unquenchable light that no darkness can ever overcome. May I be reminded that even the faintest glimmer or spark of faith and light is enough to set a blaze of glory alight in your name.

Surround them with your angel armies, and may this vision of peace be with all cancer patients.

I ask for your mighty healing in the name of Jesus, through whom we are offered the blessing of eternal life.

Amen.

Living with Treatment Routine

Father God,

I know you are a constant God who, no matter what I think or feel, will never leave my side.

How blessed I am to have you with me, Father.

My family and I are suffering much anguish about my treatment and its effects.

May the physicians and medications offer some relief to the side effects and may I feel able to cope with the days ahead.

Strengthen my steps, steady me, lead me and renew my faith in you.

May this treatment be effective and my perseverance and the power of prayer enable my healing and renewal.

I ask all this in Jesus' name.

Amen.

Prayer at Christmastime

Father God,

Thank you for the gift of your son, Jesus Christ, which we celebrate at Christmas.

You allowed yourself to live among us here in human form, vulnerable as a baby in the straw.

You allowed yourself to feel what it is to be human, out of your love for us, and so you understand the feelings of fear and despair that make our stomachs churn and our hearts race when we face huge hurdles in life.

Be with me as I face another week on my difficult journey, and be with me in my humanity, my fear, anger, despair and upset.

Remind me of the hope you gave through vulnerability, and that I too must live in hope and faith of your promise to remain as my constant companion, until I meet with you in glory.

Provide healing to my body and mind, and may I see your radiant light more clearly this week ahead.

Thank you for the blessing of my faith and for the amazing gift of your child, Jesus Christ, in whose name I pray.

Amen.

After a Much-Needed Holiday

Heavenly Father, Mighty Creator and Eternal Lord,

Thank you for my holiday, a much-needed break for me from the routine of treatments and hospitals.

May I be reminded that your hands made the sun and moon and the scale of your majesty is beyond my comprehension.

Those same hands created me as your beautiful child, an act of wonder and faith.

As you once held me in my mother's womb, so too now, hold me in those gentle hands and provide that same safety and sanctuary.

A return to home after an escape from the routine of treatment feels like a loss of freedom so longed for, a thud back into reality.

Tonight, I pray for my renewal from my holiday to encompass my days and weeks ahead at home and not just feel like a past sensation. The return needn't mean those feelings have to end; please transform that warmth of heart into renewed strength and vigour for the days ahead.

Please allow my new memories to generate smiles when needed and calm when at rest.

My home is supposed to be the place where I feel safe and secure, and more recently my home has had such times of illness and sadness that it feels oppressive. Give me the peace of knowing that a return home does not signify a return to those sad times; my illness has not changed for this return, nor has it gone for my holiday; your all-encompassing love is my constant.

If I feel like I want to run away, hold my hand and keep me standing. Remind me of the distance I have travelled on this journey so far.

Allow me to think ahead to my next holiday, and allow me to feel once again invigorated with my belief of you and my hope for healing.

None of us know what the days ahead bring, in health or in sickness, and as I think of this I pray for peaceful rest for the people who will not return home this day as they had planned.

I try to live in the now, but it is difficult, Lord, particularly with my overwhelming fears; let this wretched disease not dis-ease my resolute hope in better times ahead.

Fill my cup with your Holy Spirit so that it spills over with hope. It is so very tough, but steady me and my family, and keep me stepping forward in your light, renewed after sleep tonight.

I thank you, Lord, for your resolute and steadfast life and commitment, your light and power and your companionship in my journey ahead.

May I take each step forward in your eternal light and hope,

Amen.

Blood Transfusions

Father God,

When we are scared... comfort us.

When we are weak... strengthen us.

When we are doubtful... reaffirm our faith.

Be with me this day, as I go for my blood transfusion, Lord.

I thank you that I live in a place where these treatments are available and that you give wisdom to the medical teams to enable them to care for me.

I look towards you as I wait for the transfusion and for my strength to return.

Please help me move on from this emotionally; still my fears and ready me for my further treatment with the new blessing of strength from the transfusion.

Thank you for the kindness of those who gave this gift of blood and, with it, renewal.

When we are scared... comfort us.

When we are weak... strengthen us.

When we are doubtful... reaffirm our faith.

When we are sick... heal us.

In the name of Christ.

Amen.

Treatment Delayed

After building myself up for treatment I am scared, Lord, that I am now too weak for it to proceed.

I dread the treatment and its effects, and now I long for it to pervade my body.

Why am I so weak?

Is it getting worse?

I am so scared.

Please guide my physician, Lord, to make the right choices for my future.

May any interventions help me to regain my strength so that my treatment can proceed.

I pray this in Jesus' name.

Amen.

Last Chemo in Cycle and...

Dear Heavenly Father,

I bring myself before you tonight, and my family.

I have endured such acute treatment, Lord, and now that the last cycle of this chemo has passed, I come to give you thanks for bringing me through this most trying treatment, with the fortitude and strength that only comes from you.

Thank you that the treatment has been worthwhile and that my body is recovering from recent therapies.

Thank you, Lord, for my family and friends' fortitude in supporting me. This is a journey for them all, one without a guidebook but which can be travelled together, even at the darkest of times.

Thank you, Lord, for my children and loved ones, for their love of me and their ability to always make me smile, even on the hardest days.

As I adapt to life without chemo, give me the courage to trust this break in treatment and let me enjoy feeling stronger.

Let my hugs with my children and loved ones be long, let my companionship with my partner be loving and let my relationship with my family, who are ever there, be one of laughter and togetherness.

Let me heal.

Cast out the cancer and its wicked presence; eradicate its roots and make every cell of the cancer fade and die.

May I produce pure, strong and healthy blood, nourished by my diet. Restore all those parts made weak and make my many good cells grow stronger and stronger.

Cast your light and ever-enduring love into every cell in my body and create strength, fortitude and healing.

Thank you for hearing my prayer and thank you for being with me and my family and for your strengthened relationship with them.

You are a mighty Lord indeed, and I am in awe at your mercies, presence and creation.

In Jesus' name.

Amen.

Having a Break from Treatment

May I put my trust in my physician, just as I put my trust in you.

Without my treatment I feel so vulnerable, when I should be feeling liberated.

My routines of treatment have been the core of my existence since this cancer arrived, and they give me a semblance of control.

This gap in treatment feels like I am floating adrift, not sure of where I am heading and not knowing what lurks in the waters ready to rear its head.

May I lay back as I drift along, and fix my sight upon you.

May I listen to the calm waters of your love and may I feel your light and warmth on my face.

Help me to relax, restore and ready myself for when the waters become less calm and for when another storm appears. At times, I have felt like I have hardly caught a break in the crashing waves, and now this reprieve.

Allow me to prepare for all possibilities and strengthen my anchor.

You are my strength, shelter and ever-present guide.

May I trust in this time and in you.

Amen.

For Healing on Day of Treatment

Eternal Father,

Be with me and my family this day as I attend clinic for more treatment.

May I travel safely there, have a smooth day of treatment and be able to return home in good spirits.

I pray for healing from this treatment and by your mighty hands.

As I think of the hideous tumour, I visualise it shrinking and fading in awe of your mighty love and astounding power.

As my blood travels around my veins with the treatment today, send with it your incredible peace and new life. I ask specifically for renewal, strength and healing.

I know that you walk with me and I see this in the journey I have made so far.

You sent your son as the exception to the rules, to break the mould and to make a difference to the whole world.

I pray that my body's response to this disease follows in the hope of our heavenly Lord Jesus, by defying the odds, breaking the mould with wellness and with it the tumour's demise. I want to make a difference to others around me with my hopes of healing.

I know that these gifts are from you, Father, and on my knees, I humbly thank you for your mercies, although my words will never seem sufficient.

I believe in Jesus your son, the master of exceptions and my inspiration, and I believe in your healing power and miraculous strength that has got me as far as this today.

Praying for my miracle of healing. Amen.

For Courage

Lord,

May I face my battle armed with the gifts of your love, peace, compassion, grace and courage.

May your love be my shield,

Your peace be my fortress,

Your compassion be my clemency,

Your grace be my armour,

And your courage be my weaponry.

My prayers are my battle cry and I step forward in faith, a conqueror in my commitment to you.

Amen.

Thank You in the Storm

I praise you, Father, through this storm.

I shout my worship above the clamour;

With arms outstretched I reach to you,

With prayers for safety hour upon hour.

My heart is heavy with the burden I sustain,

And I fall on my knees in sickness and wear.

I am struggling, Lord, to see through the rain,

But I thank you through it all with this my prayer.

Amen.

Learning to Live with Uncertainty

Living in limbo is so trying, Father God.

I am neither here nor there.

I feel like I am neither living nor dead;

Static in fear, tired and weak, and while I am at this curve in the road, I cannot yet see what is around this bend, the next step on my journey of how long I will travel for.

Remind me, Father, that even when people are on a bending road, with less awareness of their journey than the healthy and well, that all paths hold uncertainty, just like my own. Assurances are present for no one and we must embrace this gift of life day by day.

Make my awakened consciousness my greatest blessing. In it the colours of life are more vivid and the gift of love unending and overwhelming.

May my uncertainty be overshadowed by the gift of my clear sight of what it means to be alive. I can see the gift of the new day, the amazing blessing of a new dawn, and I am grateful for the life you breathe in me.

May my moments with loved ones be full of your glory and spirit in the joy that they bring.

Amen.

After Chemo or Treatment

I am in a deep, dark well,

Lying on the floor at the bottom,

In pain, pitifully low, trapped, wretched and desperate.

The walls are so steep and impossibly high and the deep darkness ensnares me.

I am scared, alone and my inner screams of anguish echo through my mind.

Call to me, Lord; give me the strength that I may lift my head and look up from my misery to catch a glimpse of the light that is you.

Only you are my sanctuary and by your love and grace may I focus on the light, if only a glimmer.

As the new day rises, may that light grow, just as the sun dawns on all your creation.

Reach down to me and pull me to safety, healing and recovery.

I fix my eyes on you.

Amen.

Prayers for Renewal

Lord, you can make all things new.

Just as in the beginning you created the world, so I know that all good things come from you.

The intricacies and beauty of your world astound me, each single piece of creation in your sight and known to you.

Be with my tired body, each cell battling for survival from this disease and hurting from the difficult treatments I must bear.

Renew me, Lord, and make all things new.

Renew my spirit, Lord, and revive it.

Renew my body, Lord, and repair it.

Renew my love for you and fill me with your Holy Spirit.

Amen.

I Can Do This Again

In your majesty, I can achieve things I cannot even dream of.

In your light, I can chase my dreams of health.

In your name, I can do what is necessary, Lord.

In your arms, you will carry me through.

In your name, I pray this prayer.

You are my deliverer and my determination.

Amen.

I Cannot Do This, Lord

I could run away, leave all this behind, but I cannot escape this cancer.

I cannot do this, God; I cannot face this anymore.

No more treatment.

No more hospitals.

No more hope.

No more energy.

I have no peace and feel trapped in a living and dying hell.

I can face no more.

I can step no farther.

This cannot be.

Cradle your child, Father; whisper to me of your mercies.

Amen.

Recurrence

It cannot be.

I am so shocked and yet I am not surprised.

This nasty, lurking disease has crept back into my life, reeking of its intent.

Steady me, Lord, to face this again.

I can do all this with you.

I can face all things with you.

I can bear all things with you,

For where I am, you are too.

Amen.

Loss of Work

Lord God, Father of all,

For so long my work has been my identity and now all that has gone – and with it, it feels like a large part of me has disappeared.

I am now a patient, not a worker or employee, and I feel useless.

Your son, Jesus, was a carpenter and found himself carrying a tremendous wooden cross, thorns piercing his head.

May my loss of work not be a burden I carry; give me the gift of acceptance.

Even through the difficult path and anguish, Jesus persevered, his identity as a carpenter, then a preacher and the Messiah, and then laid low as a criminal. He was set aside with murderers and thieves and he saw them as his own flesh.

Remind me, Lord, that I am made equal to all of your children, regardless of my circumstance or my changing identity. My worth is not defined by my ability to work.

I am worthy of your love and I will praise you, Father, throughout my transformation.

Your mighty hand creates the butterflies and their beauty as they emerge from their bare and barren cocoons. May I too be reborn into your glory, name and knowledge and shine with your beauty and love.

Please transform me in your honour, Father God.

Amen.

Loss of Fertility

Father God.

My heart is broken.

My dreams are shattered.

I am low.

I feel so guilty that my body has failed and that now my partner has to suffer too, in this way.

I know they love me, Lord, but I want you to set them free if this is too much for them.

This feels like the worst insult, a violation to take away my future in this way.

Bind up my broken heart as I grieve this loss, Lord.

Be with me and my partner and comfort the broken-hearted.

Amen.

Loss of Self-Esteem

Your son stood and walked alongside the worthless and lowly, and now he draws alongside me too, God.

I feel so worthless.

I cannot do all the things I want to do and I cannot be to others what I want to be.

I know people try to help me, but the looks of strangers, however kind, can pierce. They look at me as a cancer patient, not as me. I do not want my identity to be of this wretched disease.

When I look in the mirror someone else looks back at me, a stranger, an imposter, someone I no longer know.

This person looks so worried, drawn and weak, so tired and frail.

I pity them.

Please show me signs, Lord, of who I was and who I can be.

Love me, Father, when I cannot love myself.

Amen.

Loss of Hair

This disease has stripped me of so much, Lord, and now my hair.

This is so hard.

As I look in the mirror I barely recognise myself anymore.

I thought facing this disease was tough but now this feels like a hurdle too far.

God, give me the strength to face this.

My new identity as a patient is laid bare for all to see;

No anonymity now.

The cancer has taken my health and now has taken my visual identity.

I will endure this test as I know that, when all else is stripped away, this horrid disease cannot take away you.

Forgive me, Father, for my past vanities.

Forgive me for time spent worrying about my looks instead of just living for you.

Father, please give me bravery to face this new challenge as your beautiful child, naked in my vulnerability, made in your son's image.

Amen.

Numb

I think it hurts so much physically and emotionally, I actually cannot feel anymore.

I am numb.

At times, it feels like death would be easier to bear.

My heart is broken, my body is tired and my prayers feel empty.

I am desolate.

Lord, my only hope can be found in you and so I offer up this humble prayer of brokenness and ask that you breathe life into me once again.

Allow me to feel once more, even when the sensations are desperately painful and the sorrow unfathomably deep.

You sent your son, Jesus Christ, that he could be human and flesh, that he could demonstrate love for you, Father, through pain, isolation and fear.

In his name, I commit my numb and broken self to you, in faith and in seeking forgiveness and compassion.

Amen.

Panic

I cannot catch my breath and my heart is racing.

Let me breathe in your love and breathe out my panic.

Let me breathe in your peace and breathe out my panic.

Let me breathe in your Holy Spirit and breathe out my panic.

Let me breathe in your grace and breathe out my panic.

Let me breathe, oh breath of Life.

Amen.

Weakness of Infection

I feel so weak, my heart races as it fights this infection.

If I stood I would fall.

If I was held I would crumble and fragment.

I am under.

I am broken.

I am drawing closer to you.

As I close my eyes, may my body rally against this; as I draw a breath, breathe life into me, Lord, and pull me up where I can see no way through.

I am desperate.

I am under.

Lift me, Father, carry me through,

I beg of you.

Amen.

Fluid

It is so uncomfortable and heavy,

So oppressive I can barely breathe or move.

Guide my physicians, Lord, in removing the ascites from my body, safely and without infection, that I may eat again and nourish my poor weak body, and that I may rest comfortably again and heal.

What a worry this fluid is, and how it worries my partner and my family. More worry, more treatment, more to fight through.

As I close my eyes, I feel close to you and I dive and submerge myself into the tenderness of your care.

Amen.

Sickness

The sickness is intense.

The treatment has made me so sick that I am desolate.

May my treatment be making the cancerous cells even sicker than me.

May they be obliterated by the power of the treatment and annihilated by its strength.

May my sickness fade and my body rest, and ready itself for fluids and nourishment.

I pray for my treatment to be effective and for my healing, in the name of your son, Jesus Christ.

Amen.

Education

Thank you, Father, that we live in a time and place with the medical equipment, treatments and care centres that we do.

How amazing that new treatments are being developed every day and that more and more lives are being saved!

Guide your children as physicians and researchers to find more ways to treat cancer and continue to save lives.

Give them the courage to try to develop new medicines and practices, and as I think of all the lives that have gone before without such opportunities, may I pray thanks daily for the opportunities of my treatment.

I pray, Father, that people who live in different places and are less fortunate than me in their access to treatment may have new opportunities presented to them.

I pray too, Father, for increased awareness and education of people, that they may recognise symptoms earlier and access earlier life-saving treatments with greater success rates.

How mighty you are that your children can have such knowledge and expertise, and develop medicines and treatments. These gifts come from you and I humbly thank you, Father God.

Amen.

Life After Cancer

How mighty you are!

I am saved, and my prayers can never be sufficient for my praise and honour of your majesty, your clemency and your compassion.

May my every living second sing aloud your hallelujahs and my new life be full of honour for all those who have lost their fight to this dreadful disease.

May my gift of life be a blessing to others.

I eternally praise you, Father God, Deliverer and Healer, and I am forever yours.

Amen.

Preparing to Live

Where to start?

What to do?

Everything is new, Lord;

Everything is whole.

How bright the sky, how verdant the grass, how deep and powerful your oceans!

May this journey inspire a life lived in your name.

May I be your wise disciple and may I draw alongside those in need and tell them of you, your might and power, and of this gift of life we have.

Live, love, live.

Amen.

Healing and Radical Hope

Generous and loving Father,

Surround me with your love and might.

May my treatments be conducted with wisdom, diligence and care, and provide a best outcome for me.

As the consultant makes my treatment plan may his wisdom gain the best overall effect for me.

Mostly, Lord, I give thanks for your steadfast support to me since my diagnosis. With your help, stamina and resources I have achieved so much.

I am working so hard, with the unwavering support of my family, walking forward along this battle line.

Arm me with your shield of faith against fear and anger and your heavenly weaponry of peace and healing.

I long for your faith, ultimate pure and total faith.

May my radical hopes and prayers allow your healing to grip me and hold me in the depths of your deep, deep love.

I ask all this in Jesus' name.

Amen.

Chemo or Radiation Being Effective While Taking Its Toll

Father Lord,

When I'm on my knees in pain or fear, I'm in the perfect position to pray.

I pray to you, my Holy Father, for me as your child, as my treatment is causing much pain, sickness, weakness and distress.

I pray that this treatment will destroy that ugly, wretched and unwelcome disease.

I am mindful of the pressure and pain it places on the rest of my body. It is so, so hard for me, Lord.

Please be with me now, filling my home with your Holy Spirit, and may my body become your vessel of peace, spirit and healing.

Pour into me your light, warmth, comfort and healing waters.

Protect the healthy cells, which are the majority. Empower these cells to rise up as sacred armies in your name, and move past this stage of treatment side effects to be ready for renewal over the coming days.

Pour into me your love, which transcends my knowledge.

I can never fathom the depths of your love and commitment to me, and I humbly give thanks to you.

My words can never suffice for my gratitude to you, Almighty God.

May I be reminded that my moments of doubt are when I'm actually closest to you, because they make the issue of my faith so central. Just as Thomas doubted Christ's resurrection until he saw the wounds, I am reminded of your truth, your valour and your blessings even at times I find it hard to see you.

Blessed are those who have not seen and yet believe.

I believe in you, our God; I believe in our Saviour, your son, Jesus Christ; and I believe in the Holy Spirit and the promise of heaven for me as your child.

Raise up your mighty army and fight for me this evening; raise up those healthy cells to receive repair and renewal; and raise up my heart, nearer to your light, nearer to your powerful, mighty and awesome love, for your comfort and peace.

Heal me radically.

I ask this in the name of your son, who made the lame walk, the blind see and raised the dead to life – Jesus Christ.

Amen.

For My Treatment

Heavenly Father,

As the darkness of night enfolds us, may your burning, intoxicating light shine in my body after a long and draining day of treatment.

Strengthen me as the strong and all-encompassing medicine takes hold of those nasty cancer cells, and allow the good cells around to survive and cope well with the treatment and regenerate quickly.

While the days ahead may well be tough, be the ever-present light in my hope, the clear focus in my despair and my ever-present comforter in my upset.

As the chemo destroys the cancer, may your light and love heal my body.

I thank you, Lord, for your great mercies and I humbly, on my knees, thank you for this day and the gift of tomorrow.

I pray this in the name of your precious son, Jesus Christ.

Amen.

Peace

Heavenly Father,

Be with my family, friends and me, as we are crushed in spirit.

May they and I be led to you as our refuge, our sanctuary and our everlasting peace.

Lead us in our sleep through this dark cave, out onto warm sands, with whispering seas and refreshing air, to the calm, deep and peaceful ocean, vast and immeasurable, like the waters of your peace and the depths of your love.

May we know we are loved, supported and upheld in the prayers of many people.

God of peace, dove of peace, give me the wings of your faith and peace to soar above these circumstances in prayer.

You made the world entire, you are boundless, you are endless and your peace cannot be contained.

In Jesus' name.

Amen.

Protecting Peace

Father God,

Draw close to my family, friends and me on this difficult day.

Hold us close in your long, loving embrace and be with us.

Your compassion for us is boundless and I fall on my knees in humble prayer to you to ask for your fortitude and presence to be with us, that we may know your limitless peace.

In the name of Jesus, our peacemaker.

Amen.

Surrender

I am yours, Father;

May your will be done.

I am yours, Lord,

On earth and when I see your face in heaven.

I am yours, mighty Creator,

Forever and ever.

Into your arms, I commit myself and I surrender myself to your love and glory.

Amen.

When I See Your Face

When I look upon your face, Jesus, I will be free;

No more suffering, weakness or pain.

I know that you will not leave me over these coming days.

Meet me, Lord, and carry me home.

Bring your peace and love to my family and may they know that I have found sanctuary with you.

In my Father's name, I wait for you.

Amen.

Suffering

Father God,

I can never understand why I am having to suffer this much and my heart feels broken.

I am angry, hurt and afraid.

Your son, Jesus Christ, my saviour and redeemer, suffered on the cross and called out to you. He felt forsaken and forgotten.

I know, Lord, you never left him in his trials and suffering and so too may I gain comfort knowing that your love for me is steadfast and unceasing.

You know, Lord, my pain, sickness, worry and suffering.

My tears are prayers to you when my words fail.

Remind me, Lord, that in this blackness of suffering, you are the only true light; even when I feel depleted, crushed or angry, the smallest flicker of faith remains burning, as unending and steadfast as your love.

I thank you for my life and ask that you would encircle me with your might, majesty, power and peace at this time.

May my tears be my prayers, may my fear become my determination and may my suffering become my strength.

May I feel your love and be upheld and sustained by this prayer.

May my friends and family know my love for them and your love for them too as they wait for this suffering to end for me. Draw them into the light of your faith and relationship with you and Jesus.

In the name of the redeemer, Jesus Christ, through whom I humbly receive your grace and faith and whose example makes me determined to keep my face turned to your light. Amen.

Longing to Be at Home

My home became my prison at times of treatments, and how I longed to flee and walk in the sun and fresh air!

Now, Father, in this hospital room I long to be at home once more;

No longer a prison, but a place of sanctuary and loved ones.

Fill my home with your love and peace, that my loved ones who miss me so much know of your love and light.

Comfort them in their grief and fill my empty place with your power and understanding today and in the days, weeks, months and years ahead.

Amen.

For a World Without Cancer

One day, Lord, the news will declare the cure.

One day, Lord, this suffering will be no more,

One day, Lord, cancer will have no place,

Pervading the whole entire human race.

Our hope is in you; we pray for that day.

We pray for a complete cure.

Amen.

Preparing to Die

Be with my family and friends as I take this final part of my journey.

I have longed to win, Lord.

I have longed to beat this cancer but I am so tired.

I can do this no more.

If I cannot be free of this disease, then free me through my death.

Eradicate me of my hurt, anguish, anger and sadness.

Meet me, Father, and guide me though my final days.

Draw me closer to you so that I have no fear.

Make me whole and renew me in your kingdom.

I pray for my loved ones.

May they always know my love, my gratitude for them in my life, and may they always know you in the difficult time ahead.

I am here, Lord, waiting patiently for you.

I know you are near me now.

Please forgive me, Lord, for all that I have done wrong in my life, that was not to your glory.

Let me be with you for eternity.

I am here, Lord, waiting patiently for you.

Amen.

Similar Books by the Publisher

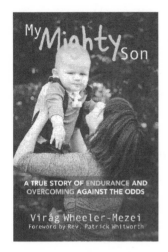

My Mighty Son
Virág Wheeler-Mezei

ISBN 978-1-911086-54-3

This is the story of a journey that few of us have to take; it is only for the bravest. Soon after Virág married James she became pregnant. Nine months later Luke was born, appearing to be a very healthy baby. And then their lives changed suddenly and drastically. Luke became unwell at around six months old. He was admitted to the local hospital and then was transferred to Bristol for radical emergency brain surgery for an aggressive brain tumour...
But this is a story of triumph in the midst of pain, frustration, bewilderment and uncertainty; of peace and confidence where normally there would be none.

Think Positive
Tammy Griffith

ISBN 978-1-910197-98-1

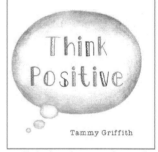

Think positive?
Easier said than done sometimes. Especially when we are in the midst of great challenges.
This book, compiled by a young woman battling a brain tumour, contains over 100 inspirational quotes, proverbs and sayings that will help you to face the unexpected.

Books available from all good bookshops and from the publisher:
www.onwardsandupwards.org